THE FOUNDING OF

THE TORCH HONOR SOCIETY

OF YALE UNIVERSITY

A Record of Peace and War

(1916–1917)

By GEORGE HENRY NETTLETON

NEW HAVEN, CONNECTICUT

1 9 5 4

The Printing-Office of the Yale University Press

We, the undersigned, agree to form ourselves into a Senior Society in the Sheffield Scientific School. It is agreed that the entire matter be kept secret until the society decides to the contrary.

S.Y. Estens, 1917 S
[signature] 1917 S
Farley Hopkins 1917 S
Graham M. Brush 1917 S
Cord Meyer 1917 S
E.S. Wilson 1917 S
Carl Wiedemann 1916 S
H. Wiley Krotzer 1917 S
C.B. Armstrong 1917 S
C.R. Slack, Jr. 1917 S
G.W.R. Crawford Jr. 1917 S
C.H. Bunker 1916 S
C.F. [illegible]
Joseph W. Roe

The Torch Agreement of November 1916.

TO THE FOUNDERS AND FOLLOWERS
OF THE TORCH HONOR SOCIETY

CONTENTS

CHAPTERS

THE FOUNDING OF
THE TORCH HONOR SOCIETY

CHAPTER I

THE SPRING TERM OF 1916

THE FIRST steps toward forming a new Honor Society in the Sheffield Scientific School of Yale University were taken during the spring term of 1916. Shortly after mid-years, two Seniors of the Class of 1916 S.—Arthur H. Bunker and Carl F. Wiedemann—and several Juniors of the Class of 1917 S.—among them, Graham M. Brush, Farley Hopkins, and Edward J. Winters—formed the nucleus of a gradually expanding group that discussed and developed the initial suggestion. From the outset it was an undergraduate project. It stemmed directly from informal but progressive discussions of the current trends and problems of University development, especially as intensified by the rapid growth in the size of Sheff classes. The pioneers of the project became quickly convinced that there was ample room and reason for a new Yale society, drawn from the entire body of Sheff upper-classmen, widely representative of diverse undergraduate activities and interests, and uniting its members in mutual endeavor to serve Yale thoughtfully and constructively. All agreed that the time was ripe for intelligent readjustments to the changing conditions within and between the University's separate Undergraduate Schools.

The broad appeal of the new project had proved instant and contagious. How best to meet its basic aim of constructive service to Yale was now, as all realized, a question for deliberate and painstaking study. To such investigation the small but ardent band of pioneers committed themselves decisively and wholeheartedly. The date of that pivotal decision is precisely fixed in the personal diary of one of the 1917 S. Torch members. In that record, maintained throughout his college course, is an arresting entry:

March 8, 1916. Torch Honor Society started.

It marks the advance of the venture from its first testing-grounds of individual opinion to the common field of decision and of concerted action. It emphasizes alike the birth and the christening of the new Yale Honor Society.

The Naming of Torch

In the constant light of the unfolding history of Torch, its inspired choice of name remains at once characteristic and prophetic. It reflects clearly the questing spirit of its founders and followers. In the christening of Torch, its sponsors adopted a universal symbol of enlightening leadership and of beneficent service. Their chosen emblem—the uplifted torch—is, in its local application, a token of ardent allegiance to the guiding creed of Yale—*Lux et Veritas.*

In designating Torch as an "Honor Society," its sponsors followed the Sheff precedent set by the Aurelian Honor Society and sanctioned by campus usage. Though their own definitions of aims and methods had, from the very start, comprehended marked departures from the current pattern, they recognized the practical advantages of accepting a general term that conveniently differentiated Sheff "Honor Societies," on the one hand, from the various Sheff fraternities and societies, and, on the other hand, from the Senior Societies of Yale College. With the christening of the Torch Honor Society, all its sponsors became in reality, as in name, equal and active partners in the mutual enterprise.

Early Plans and Progress

From the pivotal meeting of March 8, 1916, onwards, it was the challenging task of the architects of the new plan to determine its requisite specifications. During the remaining weeks between the spring vacation and final examinations they made substantial progress. The two Seniors, in disclosing their original proposal to the first Juniors consulted, had made it clear that its actual adoption and fulfillment would rest with the Juniors. Accordingly, the existing nucleus of members defined three principles to govern later additions to their numbers: (1) to set the initial quota of Juniors at *ten;* (2) to add, early in Senior year, other members from the Class of 1917 S.; (3) to make no further elections from the outgoing Class of 1916 S. All three decisions pointed ahead to the next college year as the period of active execution of the steadily maturing project. The lasting effects of the first two decisions are familiar in the settled practice of Junior elections of the "First Ten," and of fall term Senior elections to enlarge the numbers and scope of class representation. The third decision, if negatively phrased, was essentially affirmative and forward-looking. In recognizing that the mere election of a group of ten Seniors about to graduate could add little beyond nominal and momentary endorsement of the general project, full responsibility for its practical development during the coming year was placed on the group that, as Seniors, would conduct its activities. A logical sequel to the present actions was the determination to make no public announcements till next year. Apart from their immediate bearings, these early instances of purely undergraduate initiative and decision remain characteristic. During the rest of the spring term, the criteria of membership and the corresponding elections to fulfill them were matters of absorbing interest.

The Aurelian Honor Society

In establishing a second Honor Society in the Sheffield Scientific School, its founders examined carefully the precedents and policies inaugurated by the Aurelian Honor Society in 1910–1911. These immediate backgrounds are clearly visualized in the first public announcement of the founding of the "Aurelian Society," published in the *Yale Daily News,* on January 31, 1911. The official statement of aims and qualifications for membership is given in explicit detail:

It has long been felt by many members of the Sheffield Scientific School that there was need of more adequate recognition in Senior year of those qualities and achievements now rewarded imperfectly, or not at all, by the existing social and scientific organizations in the School. To meet this need there was founded by members of 1910 S. an open honorary organization known as the Aurelian Society. Its membership is composed of those men who have, during their course, achieved distinction in one or more lines of undergraduate activities, literary, administrative, religious, athletic, dramatic, or debating, and at the same time have maintained a high grade of scholarship and character. Seven men are chosen from the incoming Senior Class at the end of Junior year. Three new honorary members are elected at the same time, and are taken from among the alumni of the School, or from those who have achieved prominence in the world of education or public affairs. A public lecture is given each year by an eminent man on some subject of general interest.

If the aim of the founders of the Society is realized, men will come to see more and more the importance and advantages of maintaining a high standard of scholarship and manly conduct together with their other college activities.

Then follows a list of members—six honorary, seven from the previous Class of 1910 S., and seven from the current Senior Class of 1911 S.—in evident accord with the declared principles and methods of selection.

The next half-decade, during which Aurelian remained as the sole Honor Society, emphasized its unique position in the Sheff social system. Its awards of membership, early characterized by the *Yale News* as "Sheff's Reward for Merit," and the initial stress laid officially on high scholastic standing as a fixed requirement had suggestions of kinship with Phi Beta Kappa and Sigma Xi rather than with the Senior Societies of Yale College. Within the Sheff fraternities and societies, the main reservoir from which the Honor Society drew its members, the practical effects of its policies were closely viewed and discussed. Together with ready recognition of its high standards of selection, it was increasingly felt that they involved questionable sacrifices in breadth of membership and influence. Until the close of Senior year, when three to five outgoing Seniors were added, class representation was confined solely to the seven men elected late in Junior year.

From the wider standpoints of the general interests of Sheff, criticism tended to focus on the rigid scholastic requirements which excluded from the field of candidacy many whom class and campus recognized as outstanding and influential leaders. That such criticism was well-founded was reflected, within the course of the next few years, in the Honor Society's gradual abatements of the scholastic standards initially set. Thus, for example, the original (1911) phrase, "a high grade of scholarship," was successively modified—in 1913, to "a reasonably high grade of scholarship," and in 1914, to "a satisfactory stand in scholarship." Such quiet de-emphasis, however, was too gradual to attract the general attention which the campus had given to the incisive original statement, or to counteract persistent impressions of undue narrowing of the field of candidacy.

By 1916, two generations of Sheff students (under the then existing three-year Sheff system) had seen the novelty of an open (non-secret) Honor Society give way to appreciation of its durable qualities. Tangible signs of such recognition appeared in the questionnaires and Class Books of 1916 S. and 1917 S. in their records of "Preferences in regard to the respective values of a 'Y', Sigma Xi, an Aurelian Key, and a *News* badge." These indications of prevalent campus opinion are of pertinent interest since the founders of Torch were themselves members of the given Sheff classes. Though the "Y" and Sigma Xi remain, in both years, emphatic first and second choices, and together attract all save a slender remnant of the total votes, it is significant that the emblem of the Sheff Honor Society has been accorded open consideration with long-established and valued symbols of campus distinction. Its influence as a mark of individual attainment, if as yet comparatively slight, was nevertheless suggestive. The founders of Torch, familiar with these current trends of upper-class opinion, found them mainly encouraging. They felt that by 1916 the campus had come to regard the Honor Society as an established institution, and had, at least to an appreciable degree, endorsed it. No less surely did they feel that the evidence pointed the need and opportunities of widening the current conception of an Honor Society, and of improving its general standing and service in the community.

The Sheff Fraternities and Societies

Besides the primary relation of Torch to Aurelian as a Sheff Honor Society, the founders of Torch thoroughly discussed its relations to the Sheff fraternities and general societies. Together, these various units constituted the Sheff Interfraternity system, whose Council functioned mainly in regulating joint agreements as to times and methods of elections. Factional disputes and animosities were unhappily frequent and persistent. The founders of Torch sensed the possibilities of aiding, collectively as well as individually, in bettering conditions that militated against the best interests not alone of the societies but of the general undergraduate body. Their own adoption of ten (instead of seven) as the initial unit of membership and of class representation was an early step to enlarge the bases of mutual understanding and of constructive service to the common undergraduate interests. Its molding influence, first shaped within the Torch circle, then doubly attested in the Joint Agreements of the two Sheff Honor Societies, has been an abiding factor of accord throughout the entire course of their eventual development as University Honor Societies.

In filling the quota of the "First Ten" from 1917 S., the gradually expanding Torch group stressed not merely individual achievement and influence but group coöperation. The giving and acceptance of its elections were conditioned on firm adherence to its central aim of collective service to the general welfare. The successive individual responses thus directly heightened group unity and confidence. The principle of unity in diversity had other consistent bearings and results. Among many elements of distributional strength, the Torch group considered existing Junior class affiliations with the separate Sheff fraternities and societies, guarding, on the one hand, against undue recognition of any single interest and, on the other hand, against automatic inclusion of every organization within the Sheff Interfraternity circle. With the rounding out of its "First Ten," Torch secured substantial range and balance in the social, as in the many other, aspects of distributional strength. Its first Junior class group comprised members from five separate Sheff fraternities and societies—Berzelius ("Colony"), Book and Snake ("Cloister"), Chi Phi ("York Hall"), Delta Phi ("St. Elmo"), and Delta Psi ("St. Anthony"). Though the breadth and strength of its composite membership were most importantly evidenced in the full field of undergraduate activities, its various links with the general Sheff social system gave to Torch added factors of internal harmony and of external influence.

The end of the spring term of 1916 closed the first of the two main periods in the founding of Torch. The "project" undertaken in March had now been carried forward decisively. The appeal of its central principles had been tested repeatedly and convincingly. From its small nucleus, the Torch membership had steadily grown in numbers and in cohesive spirit. The successful completion of its first basic unit of ten Juniors had demonstrated its organic strength. Equally deliberate and progressive were the steps that had determined the relations of Torch to general undergraduate interests and, specifically, to the existing Sheff social system. With the definite attainment, prior to the close of the spring term, of their immediate objectives, the founders of Torch faced forward confidently to the coming academic year.

CHAPTER II

THE FALL TERM OF 1916

THE SECOND and final period in the founding of Torch began with the reopening of college in September, 1916. With their return as Seniors, the "First Ten" members of the 1917 S. group resumed the Torch "project" actively. Consolidated in numbers and spirit, and encouraged by the definite gains of the spring term, they now made consistent progress. Alike in questions of external policy and in those of internal development, the central principle of constructive Yale service remained the motivating force. Its special applications may best be reviewed in the light of changing conditions in the general University environment and outlook.

The Omens of War

The June Commencement week of 1916 had instantly and dramatically linked the Yale campus with a sudden crisis in national affairs. On June 18, in the face of threatening Mexican hostilities, President Wilson ordered the immediate mobilization of the National Guard, with every prospect of dispatch to the Mexican border. Under that order were included, as part of the Connecticut National Guard, the four "Yale Batteries" of Field Artillery, comprising nearly five hundred undergraduates enlisted, in the fall of 1915, and thereafter trained in anticipation of possible American involvement in the European War. With the disbanding, by June 15, of the Yale Batteries for the normal summer vacation, their student members, save for the Seniors about to graduate, were widely scattered throughout the country. On the morning of June 20, nevertheless, the first mobilization roll call, held on campus, signalized the quick response of the Yale Batterymen to the unexpected call to the colors. It was the dramatic prologue foreshadowing the march of events that, within the course of the coming year, transformed the Yale campus into a Campus Martius.

The Interlude of Peace

When college reopened in the fall, the immediate prospects were reassuring. The threats of Mexican hostilities had soon subsided. The four Yale Batteries, after a summer of intensive training at the Field Artillery camp at Tobyhanna, Pennsylvania, had been mustered out of active service just in time for undergraduates to rejoin their classes at Yale. If, however, the "summer campaign of Tobyhanna" seemed a closed incident, its abiding influence was presently visualized in dramatic fashion. On Saturday afternoon, October 21, the Yale Bowl was given over to the presentation of the impressive *Yale Pageant,* commemorating the "Two Hundredth Anniversary of the Removal of Yale College to New Haven," and reënacting, with a cast of 6,000 representatives of City and College, historic scenes in the development of New Haven and of Yale University. To its patriotic scenes of the American Revolution and of the Civil War, this Yale Pageant of War and Peace added a stirring conclusion. Its final "modern" scene, enacted by members of the Yale Batteries, showed two firing batteries, stripped for action, and operating as if suddenly engaged on the firing line. The Yale Pageant thus set Yale's historic past and her enduring tradition of national service in vivid and vital relation to her challenging present.

During the rest of the fall term, Yale undergraduate life mainly resumed its normal ways. The reëlection of President Wilson in November reaffirmed, at least for the time being, American neutrality in the European conflict. The processes of converting the Yale Batteries into the R.O.T.C. and of developing other forms of military training—such, for early example, as the first Yale Naval Aviation unit—were gradual and unhurried. The next few months proved, accordingly, a relatively tranquil period, during which the usual peace-time activities of the campus were carried on uninterruptedly. In this brief interlude the founding of Torch became an accomplished fact.

The Progress of the Torch Project

In early October, the reassembled 1917 S. Torch group decided that the time had come to submit their project, thus far developed wholly by undergraduate initiative, to the test of independent and impartial judgment. As the first means to that end, they consulted Professor Joseph W. Roe, 1895 S., who had joined the Sheff faculty, in 1906, as instructor in Mechanical Engineering. He was doubly qualified as adviser by a full decade of Sheff teaching and by long familiarity with extra-curriculum activities. As a Sheff undergraduate he had been a founder of the *Yale Scientific Monthly,* and an editor both of the *Yale Banner* and of the *Yale Record,* and ever since his return to Yale had been active in campus and community interests. To the new Sheff enterprise he now generously lent his mature counsel and creative energy.

The import of these October conferences with Professor Roe is vividly recalled in the account by Graham Brush, one of the pioneers of the Torch project.

Several of our group called upon Joe Roe to tell him what we had been thinking about, and to ask him if he agreed with our conclusion that such an organization as we proposed was really needed in Sheff. Our objective, as we explained, was to bring together a group of men who held responsible positions in the undergraduate affairs of the University to discuss and help solve problems of the University and, more particularly, of the Sheffield Scientific School. This common purpose had already attracted and united our group and was, we felt, insufficiently served by existing Sheff organizations. We were immediately subjected to many searching questions. Joe wanted to find out whether this was a "sour grapes" group of men who were not qualified for Aurelian. He foresaw certain conflicts which might be detrimental to the interests of the University and Sheff, if that were the case. We assured him that we had no thoughts of duplicating or disturbing the current activities of other undergraduate organizations. We realized fully that we lacked the prestige and traditions of the well-established societies, and what we were looking for was not individual social distinction but a chance to work together, as a group, towards better understanding and service of Yale interests. While admitting to Joe that our motives might be questioned, we persuaded him that we were determined to stand up under any barrage of brick bats, keeping our mouths closed and letting results determine the issue.

When Joe was convinced that the group was not seeking honors for themselves, but wanted to give their services in the most effective way to the University, he immediately pledged his help and asked for a few days to consult with one of his old friends, Professor Henry B. Wright, '98, of the Yale College faculty, with whom Joe had talked on several occasions regarding the problems and proper functions of Senior Societies at Yale. Shortly thereafter, the whole group met with Joe to hear his views regarding certain principles which should be followed. Most, if not all, of his recommendations were adopted as progress was made in setting up the organization.

We decided that the Society should not be a secret society—that it would be stronger if we unanimously agreed to keep our affairs to ourselves only as each man's conscience and judgment dictated. We decided that the respect which each man held for his colleagues and his Society should be the factor for determining what should be said to others.

Joe pointed out that such respect gave strength to an organization in other important ways and that the greatest respect for one another would be attained only when each man knew himself as his colleagues knew him. Accordingly, each man must learn to know his colleagues as intimately as he knew his inward self—their weaknesses, their strength, their past failures and successes, their temptations and ambitions, their yardsticks of conduct in their daily lives. What we later called "Criticisms" was the mechanism or means by which the members could learn to know one another so thoroughly as to bind the group into a solid unit. To accomplish that result it was decided that the membership should continue to be limited to the basic unit of ten Juniors, with the proviso that two more classmates would be elected in Senior year.

This engrossing narrative of events, amply verified by other participants, recaptures the pervading spirit as well as the detail of the October conferences with Professor Roe. His progressive rôles as inquisitor, consulting architect, and master builder of the Torch project stand forth luminously. Such response no less clearly reveals the convincing strength and sincerity of the undergraduate proposals. In such free and full accord, all concerned in the conferences, in honor preferring one another, deepened mutual faith and confidence in the common enterprise.

In November, the Torch project was again notably advanced by like consultations with a second member of the Sheff faculty, Professor Carl F. Schreiber, of the German department. In him the Senior group recognized an invigorating teacher and organizer of humanistic studies in Sheff, and found a discerning and devoted counselor. His hearty approval of their plans promptly brought him into active partnership in all their concerns. Here again, the relationship between undergraduates and faculty was too instinctive to need or receive formal definition. Without constraint of action and without designation of title as "faculty advisers" or "honorary members," Joe Roe and Carl Schreiber entered the counsels and active fellowship of Torch.

The Agreement of November, 1916

Definitely linked with the November conferences is the earliest written agreement signed by the founders of Torch. This unique and characteristic document is the sole extant 1916 record individually attested by all the founders. It is a handwritten memorandum, drawn up in the briefest terms since it chiefly served to validate the cumulative list of members constituting the full group of founders. The list of fourteen comprises the two members of 1916 S., the "First Ten" of 1917 S., and the two faculty members. The entire document, with personal signatures, reads thus:

We, the undersigned, agree to form ourselves into a Senior Society in the Sheffield Scientific School. It is agreed that the entire matter be kept secret until the society decides to the contrary.

S. W. Atkins, 1917 S.
E. J. Winters, 1917 S.
Farley Hopkins, 1917 S.
Graham M. Brush, 1917 S.
Cord Meyer, 1917 S.
E. S. Munson, 1917 S.
Carl Wiedemann, 1916 S.
H. Wiley Krotzer, 1917 S.
C. B. Armstrong, 1917 S.
C. R. Black, Jr., 1917 S.

J. W. R. Crawford, Jr., 1917 S.
A. H. Bunker, 1916 S.
C. F. Schreiber
Joseph W. Roe

This written agreement, arresting in its brevity and simplicity, harks back to the unwritten but decisive agreement, at the pivotal meeting of March 8, 1916, when the pioneers of the project jointly resolved to found a new Sheff society. The November document attested the formal consolidation of the entire group of founders, without need of reviewing intervening processes that were familiar to all its members, or of anticipating the results of conferences still in progress. All parties to the agreement were recognized as equal partners, for neither then nor subsequently did the group of founders appoint officers or divide its membership into formal categories. Such instinctive community of interest and equality of responsibility were fitly symbolized in the *circle* which presently became an integral part of the chosen *emblem* of Torch.

The Torch Emblem

Intimately linked with the fall term's history was the adoption of the *Torch emblem*. In the midst of a general discussion of an appropriate badge of membership, the practical problem was solved suddenly and convincingly. On the spur of the moment, Professor Roe, an expert draftsman, quickly sketched on the back of an envelope a design embodying the three characteristic symbols of the Torch device. Then and there, as the event was to prove, he set the changeless pattern of the Torch emblem. As the central symbol, he placed the uplifted *Torch,* with its ardent flame pointing upwards—token of enlightening leadership and of beneficent service. As the second symbol, he chose the broad *circle*—token of equal and comprehending comradeship in the mutual endeavor—and made it the basic support of the *Torch.* As the third symbol, he took the numeral X—marking the initial class unit of *ten* adopted by the founders—and set it firmly across and within the broad circle encompassing and integrating the central design.

As Joe Roe's rapidly completed sketch passed from hand to hand for close study, the response was instant and enthusiastic. All admired the symmetry and force of the main structural plan, the skill of the creative artist. Above all, they felt the sensitive interpretation of the vital spirit of the Torch project. From the very start—as the record of the initial meeting on March 8 attests—the name and symbolism of the Torch had stirred the thought and imagination of its first sponsors. Now, the two added symbols bore witness to the fulfilled number of the "First Ten" and to the completed circle of the founders. Before the close of the meeting, Joe Roe's tentative sketch was unanimously approved as the Torch emblem. Unaltered even in detail, it was transmitted to the engraver as the design for the individual badges of membership and, eventually, for the Torch plaque.

In the dramatic history of Torch, the signature of the written agreement of the founders and their adoption of the official insignia of the Society are characteristic scenes. Against the fall term backgrounds, both incidents dramatize simply but vividly the course of current events. Both have left tangible memorials that together document and visualize historic actions. Yet their deepest revelation is not of the outward aspects of dramatic history. Beyond their fidelity to the fact, both scenes make manifest the incarnate and quickening spirit of the Torch enterprise.

December Decisions

During October and November, 1916, the steady progress of internal development within the Torch circle had been furthered by the nearly normal conditions of undergraduate life. Not until after the Thanksgiving holiday, which happily followed the climax of a signally victorious football season, did the campus give priority to graver issues, local and national. In December, plans for the Yale Field Artillery Unit of the R.O.T.C. were maturing, and were advanced by faculty endorsement on December 21. Their direct impact on the student body, however, was felt only with the official announcement, early in January, 1917, which defined the terms of individual application and selection for enrollment in the new R.O.T.C. Unit. Even then, its limitation of numbers to 220 narrowed the field of actual participation. Meanwhile, an evident sign of the trend of the times was the Yale Artillery Armory, given by Yale alumni, and already in process of erection on the Yale athletic playing fields adjacent to the Yale Bowl.

The founders of Torch, anticipating gradual changes in the general outlook, resolved to act forehandedly. When they reassembled after the Thanksgiving recess, the questions of the hour were merely of war-preparedness, national and local, in its tentative stages. The ultimate question of American entrance into the European War remained problematic, not imminent. In mid-December, indeed, the German peace overtures to the Allies and President Wilson's prompt reaffirmation of American neutrality seemed, at least for the moment, reassuring. Fortunately the December decisions of the Torch group rested on more than momentary grounds. Ere long, the wisdom and foresight of their provisions were to be demonstrated openly and conclusively.

In early December, the Torch Seniors decided that their best course of action was to consolidate the gains of the closing year and to safeguard their project against the uncertainties of the coming months by electing their successors from the Junior class before the Christmas vacation. This plan gave time for deliberate choice of the "First Ten" from 1918 S., and removed the risks of hasty action under pressure of some sudden emergency. It likewise provided crucial tests of the individual and independent reactions of representative Juniors to a project wholly unknown to the campus. Whether they would support it, especially in the face of altering campus conditions, remained to be seen. The Torch project had been conceived and developed to meet the circumstances and needs of peace. Reviewing it now from other angles, the Torch founders were agreed that its central principle of purposeful Yale service would, if militant need arose, be fulfilled in deep accord with the Yale tradition of national service in war. Facing an uncertain New Year, they were certain, at least, of the wisdom of preparedness for the issues whether of peace or of war.

By mid-December, the Torch Seniors determined the list of the "First Ten" from 1918 S. and, in accordance with previously decided policy, chose two additional Seniors to complete the 1917 S. group. The definite acceptance of these various elections justified, in fullest measure, the faith of the founders in their project and assured its continuity. Since the membership of the new society for the coming year was now fully established, the Torch Seniors decided to announce the results of the December elections without delay. Their chosen form of announcement was characteristic. They chose to make it merely a statement of facts in their simplest and most immediate terms, without indicating their own part in the accomplished results. Accordingly, on December 19, they gave the official list of December elections to the *Yale Daily News* for publication prior to the Christmas vacation.

DECEMBER ANNOUNCEMENTS

(a) *Yale Daily News*, December 20, 1916

On Wednesday, December 20, 1916, the *Yale Daily News* published the first official Torch announcement, disclosing the establishment of a new Sheff Honor Society. The complete list of the December elections gave the campus its first knowledge of the existence of the new organization. The Torch statement of facts appeared in a leading *News* article which summarized its main content in arresting headlines:

HONORARY SOCIETY OF THE TORCH ANNOUNCES ELECTIONS
SHEFFIELD SCIENTIFIC SCHOOL SENIOR SOCIETY TAKES TWELVE MEN

Two Men Are Elected From the Senior Class and
Ten From the Junior Class Accept Election for
the Ensuing Year

Immediately following this caption came the Torch announcement. It read thus:

The new Senior Honorary Society of the Torch of the Sheffield Scientific School announces the election from the Senior class of:

Anthony Donald Bullock, of Cincinnati, Ohio
Charles Mortimer Sheldon, Jr., of Joplin, Mo.

The following Juniors have accepted election for the ensuing year:

Robert Scott Bingham, of Methuen, Mass.
John Timothy Callahan, of Lawrence, Mass.
Harold D. Carey, of Hartford, Conn. ·
Charles Aloysius Comerford, of Brookline, Mass.
Thomas Nast Crawford, of New Rochelle, N.Y.
Chester James LaRoche, of Dorchester, Mass.
Alvan Macauley, Jr., of Detroit, Mich.
Arthur Ralston Page, of San Francisco, Calif.
Kenneth Rose Smith, of Patchogue, L.I., N.Y.
Northam Lancaster Wright, of Centerbrook, Conn.

The *News* article concluded with a brief note of tentative comment:

This new secret society, it is supposed, was started last year, when certain members of last year's Senior class induced several members of the Class of 1917 S. to establish it. The first official announcement of its existence, however, was given last night, when the elections, published above, were made public.

Though the summarizing headlines of the *News* were in strict accord with the facts, the supposition that the Torch was a "secret society" was unintentionally misleading. Evidently its designation as an "Honorary Society" had not sufficed to guard against hasty misapprehension. The Torch Seniors had other evidence that, in confining their statement to the immediate facts, they had over-simplified it. In announcing their December elections without listing those who had given them, they had omitted basic facts of vital connection. In excluding all references to themselves, they had given no indication of the numbers and distributional strength of the "First Ten" of the 1917 S. group. Since their main concern, for weeks past, had been to establish the continuity of the Torch project, they had instinctively pointed their announcement towards the crucial year ahead. They had rightly judged that the published facts would speak for themselves—for the campus was quick to recognize the comprehensive strength and range of the given elections—but they now realized that their own reticence as to the total Senior membership had left some ground for mis-

taken inferences of secrecy. To dispel such casual impressions before they gained currency, the Torch took prompt steps to supply
the missing facts.

(b) *Yale Alumni Weekly,* December 29, 1916

As the next issue of the *Yale News* would not appear until college reopened in January, whereas the *Yale Alumni Weekly* continued publication throughout the Christmas vacation, the Torch
announcement was revised for the December 29 issue of the
Weekly. This amended official statement read as follows:

The formation has been announced of the new Senior Honorary
Society of the Torch, of the Sheffield Scientific School, with the following members from the Senior Class:

Chauncey Bennett Ozier Armstrong, of Crafton, Pa.
Samuel Wright Atkins, of Marietta, Pa.
Clinton Rutherford Black, Jr., of New York City
Graham Manvel Brush, of Greenwich, Conn.
Anthony Donald Bullock, of Cincinnati, Ohio
John William Roy Crawford, Jr., of New Rochelle, N.Y.
Farley Hopkins, of Chicago, Ill.
Henry Wiley Krotzer, of Winchester, Tenn.
Cord Meyer, of Great Neck, L.I., N.Y.
Edwin Shepherd Munson, of Milford, Conn.
Charles Mortimer Sheldon, Jr., of Joplin, Mo.
Edward James Winters, of Holyoke, Mass.

The following Juniors have accepted elections for the ensuing year:

[Here were listed the "First Ten" of 1918 S., as given in the
Yale News, December 20, 1916.]

The new organization is a non-secret society which was started last
year by certain members of 1916 S., then the Senior Class. The first
official announcement of its existence, however, was given out last
week.

The two noteworthy betterments effected in the revision of
December 29 were these: (1) the inclusion of the full list of the
Senior members; (2) the explicit designation of Torch as "a non-

secret society." Both additions were constructive and character-istic. The first identified the ten Seniors of the active group simply by listing them, without distinctive emphasis, in the composite list of the twelve 1917 S. members. The second addition—the postscript to the complete Senior and Junior lists—provided a definite statement of fact to offset the misleading conjecture that the new Honorary Society was a "secret society." Both in its original and in its revised form, the Torch announcement re-mained a statement of facts, without accompanying manifesto of program that might shortly be interrupted, partly or wholly, by the militant march of events.

The Torch Seniors, who had themselves been left free to de-velop the project, as they saw fit, had faith that their successors, given like freedom and responsibility, would carry forward in like spirit. Facing the precarious future, they limited their an-nouncements to results now definitely attained. In so doing, they assured themselves and their new partners in the Torch enter-prise equal freedom of action in meeting whatever issues and emergencies the coming year might present. The announcements of December 20 and 29, 1916, brought to an eventful close the calendar year that had initiated the Torch project.

CHAPTER III

THE WINTER TERM OF 1917

THE NEW year of 1917 opened auspiciously for the Torch. The December elections had doubled its active membership and potential strength. The impact of the published lists had been instant and striking. So rapid, indeed, had been the spread of undergraduate interest that the Torch Seniors deemed it needless to republish in the *Yale News* the full lists of Senior and Junior members already made available in the *Yale Alumni Weekly*. The general recognition of the widely representative character of the Torch membership quickly placed the new Honor Society in central relation to the Sheff social system and to the broader concerns of the campus. The Sheff community was naturally inclined to welcome a new organization which obviously emphasized comprehensive rather than partisan interests, and united so many responsible and influential leaders of undergraduate activities and opinion. Independent testimony that such early and favorable impressions continued strong is given in the contemporary chronicle of events of Senior year included in the *History of the Class of 1917 S.:*

The founding of a new Honor Society, The Torch, came as a surprise to 1917 and soon made its influence felt by the loftiness of its aims and the strength of its personnel.

The Torch Delegations of 1917 S. and 1918 S.

In the first instance, as in the last analysis, the general campus verdict rested directly on the strength of the Torch personnel, as disclosed in the December announcements. In "letting results determine the issue," the Torch Seniors had consistently submitted the case to the independent judgment of the campus, unurged by special interpretation or special pleading. Individually and collectively, the Senior and Junior lists stood strictly on their own merits.

In January, 1917, the greatest common factor in campus ap-
praisal of the Torch personnel was its prominence in widely rang-
ing extra-curriculum activities. This common factor of accord
was doubly influential in a period chiefly marked by sharp differences between the Sheffield Scientific School and Yale College.
Each School was mainly a law unto itself. Each zealously guarded
its own tradition of independent origin and custom. Each maintained its separate scholastic and social life, set its own entrance requirements, organized and administered its own curriculum, developed its own building and dormitory systems and its own code
of discipline, and recruited its own faculty, with scant heed to the
other. The undergraduate body was a house divided against itself.
The two rival clans, Sheff and Academic, though by no means so
hostile as the Houses of Montague and Capulet, remained clannish.
From the common meeting-ground of Varsity athletics they with-
drew largely to their separate strongholds and local interests. The
relatively rigid three-year program of Sheff *versus* the much freer
elective system of the College, the three-year Sheff fraternities
and societies *versus* the Academic Junior and Senior societies, and
the Sheff "Honor System" *versus* the College proctoring system
in the conduct of examinations are but varied instances of lines of
cleavage that might be readily extended. Even in the reconciling
field of open extra-curriculum activities, such as athletics and the
Yale News, the extra year of experience counted heavily in favor
of College students in the competitions and final choices for posts
of leadership. Sheff Varsity captains were the notable exceptions
that proved the rule. Under such unequal and generally adverse
conditions, the signal achievements and influence of Torch members in University affairs were the salient factors that determined
and continued the favorable undergraduate verdict on the new
Honor Society.

Torch in Varsity Athletics

Campus interest in the Torch lists was intensified by the evidences
of unusual strength in the dominant field of Varsity athletics.
Among the Torch Seniors were the two Sheff captains of major

teams—Clinton R. ("Cupe") Black, of the football eleven, and
Cord Meyer, of the crew—and the two Varsity managers from
Sheff—Edward J. ("Eddie") Winters, the baseball manager, and
Chauncey Armstrong, the crew manager. These signs of leader-
ship were further evident in the choice of Cord Meyer as chairman
of the Yale Undergraduate Athletic Association, and of Eddie
Winters as one of the two undergraduate members of the Board
of Control of University Athletics, recently created by the Yale
Corporation.

The official establishment of the Board of Control, uniting
representatives of the University Administration, the Deans and
other faculty members of the two Undergraduate Schools, and
alumni and undergraduates active in various athletic fields marked
a new era in the history of Yale athletics. In readjustments to the
novel changes of policy and practice, the intelligent coöperation
of accredited student leaders was an integral force. Though the
Torch announcements were unaccompanied by formal declaration of its aim to aid in the furtherance of University affairs, the
student body was quick to connect the new Honor Society with
practical service to University athletic concerns, in the kindred
fields of conference, administration, and individual leadership. In
retrospect, that formative period in the history alike of the Board
of Control and of the Torch Honor Society suggests not merely
timely coincidence but also a happy augury. Then and thence-
forth, constructive service to Yale athletics became a firmly based
Torch tradition.

The firm maintenance of Torch representation in Yale athletics
was obvious in the December elections from the Class of 1918 S.
Four of the "First Ten" Juniors were the four Sheff Juniors in the
regular line-up of Captain Black's victorious eleven. An independent comment in the 1918 S. Class Book may here supply
backgrounds and local color of the period:

Our Class was ably represented on the championship Football Team
of 1916 by "Charlie" Comerford, "Bill" Carey, "Tim" Callahan, and
"Chet" LaRoche. The work of this quartet brought tears to the eyes

of Percy Haughton by beating Harvard for the first time since the
good old days of "Ted" Coy.

Comerford and Carey, it may be added, were promising pitchers
for the coming baseball season, while Arthur Page was a Varsity
oarsman. Thus, while for the time being, the campus mainly reviewed the Torch lists in the current light of football, it comprehended also the prospects for other major sports, especially rowing and baseball. Though secondary factors, such as Freshman and
minor sports, added details to the composite picture, the widest
undergraduate interest lay in intercollegiate athletics. In that common field, and in common accord, Yale College and Sheff recognized the breadth and the worth of the Torch contributon.

Other Extra-Curriculum Activities

In extra-curriculum activities other than athletics, the Torch lists
were likewise widely representative. The *Yale Daily News* was
represented by Farley Hopkins, a Senior editor, and by Thomas
Crawford, a Junior editor. These successive Torch elections were
doubly significant at a period when few Sheff men "made the
News," and they retain historic interest as the earliest links in the
chain of events that have led the campus, nowadays, to regard
the characteristic connections of Torch with the *News* as a well-
established post-War tradition. Tom Crawford was an editor,
also, of the *Scientific Monthly* and managing editor of the *Yale
Record,* but it was the Torch representation on the *News* that
counted more broadly in the general field of undergraduate
journalism and affairs.

In the distinct province of Sheff organizations, both general and
class, Torch was signally represented. Among Torch Seniors, for
example, Roy Crawford was chairman of the Sheff Student
Council and class treasurer; Graham Brush, a member of the Student Council, and of the Senior Prom and Class Book committees; Sam Atkins, of the Interfraternity Council and of the
Y.M.C.A. executive committee; Farley Hopkins, of the Senior
Council and of the Undergraduate Discipline Committee con-

trolling the Sheff "Honor System" of examinations; while Eddie
Winters was elected Floor Manager of the Senior Prom and Tony
Bullock headed the Yale Industrial Committee concerned with
welfare work. In due course, the Sheff constituency entrusted
like posts of responsibility and individual leadership to incoming
Torch Juniors, as when "Chet" LaRoche was chosen as head of
the Sheff Student Council, and Al Macauley as president of the
Sheff Y.M.C.A. and chairman of the Interfraternity Council. As
the new year of 1917 progressed, such signs of community service
and recognition multiplied.

Torch and the Sheff Social System

The distributional strength of Torch manifest throughout the
full range of campus activities was equally evident in the breadth
of its relations to the existing Sheff social system. In its Junior as
in its Senior group, the Torch notably combined many leaders
highly influential in their respective fraternities and societies. The
impact of such marked integration of divergent interests, especially
at a time when the clash of partisan elements had become menac-
ing, was arresting and salutary. Within the general membership
of the separate Sheff fraternities and societies, the impress of the
new Sheff Honor Society was widely felt and commended. Its
advent, indeed, was rapidly recognized as a progressive and reconciling factor in the betterment of the existing Sheff social system.

An early instance of open and extensive commentary on the
founding of Torch appeared in the *Yale News* on January 10, 1917,
as a Communication to the Chairman. Its opening paragraphs
read as follows:

The inevitable founding of another Honor Society, for several years
threatened by the very nature of the social structure in Sheff, has at
last occurred. The distinction between the two Sheff Honor Societies
is so important and so intersting in the light of the development of
the society system in Yale, that I beg leave to suggest its significance
to the University.

Here we have had one Honor Society—the Aurelian—which picked
but seven men from the Junior class and from three to five men from

the Senior class, all upon qualifications so high and so exclusive that many of the best men were unrecognized. There was a need in Sheff for an Honor Society, not of secondary importance exactly (for no order of rank can be determined without a common set of values) but which should be a little more "popular" than the Aurelian and perhaps not have such high qualifications. (I use the word "high" only in its accepted sense, and do not mean to infer, with the conventional fallacy, that the words "high," "low," "noble," etc. have any eternal validity at all, but merely indicate judgments according to inherited standards.) This need, if I may be permitted to turn prophet, will be filled by the Honor Society of the Torch. It will probably be broader, more in-clusive, more popular, more tolerant, and have a greater universality of spirit than the Aurelian, which must always be limited by the claims of its ideal. The Aurelian will be more conservative, more exclusive, less "social," and be backed by the weight of tradition, the dignity of greater age, and the sympathy of the Faculty. Both Societies are needed in Sheff: they should not be competitive, but supplementary.

In the rest of his article the writer developed other points of contrast, maintaining that "the Aurelian type is more an Academic type; the Torch, a Sheff type," and that such differentiation "will be true as long as Sheff preserves its individuality," and "until Sheff and Academic merge into one (which they probably never will)." The final paragraph congratulated the Torch "on being (contrary to the deduction of the NEWS) non-secret" and on its judgment in setting aside the "protection and power" of mystery.

Though the generalizations and prophecies thus openly ven-tured were to be largely discounted in the advancing experience of later decades, it should be recalled that the *News* communica-tion voiced points of view widely shared prior to the advent of Torch. The radical differences, organic as well as social, between the two Undergraduate Schools had long been matters of common acceptance. Faculty, alumni, and undergraduates generally dis-missed the merger of Sheff with Yale College as, at most, a re-mote possibility. None then foresaw that the Honor Societies founded in Sheff would, with their ultimate broadening into Uni-versity Honor Societies, become prophets and reconciling agents of the movement culminating, at long last, in the University's decisive consolidation, in 1944–1945, of Yale College and the Sheffield Scientific School. Such promising signs of social progress as the campus of January, 1917, saw in the founding of a new Honor Society were naturally viewed principally in their unmistakable bearings on the existing Sheff social system.

The Yale R.O.T.C. and the Naval Training Unit
(January–February, 1917)

On January 13, 1917, official announcement of definite provisions for the immediate establishment of the Yale Reserve Officers' Training Corps marked a decisive turn in the tide of undergraduate affairs. At a mass meeting which filled the auditorium of Lampson Lyceum Hall, Captain Danford disclosed the detailed plans already approved by the War Department and by the Yale Faculty, and the individual qualifications and class quotas that would determine admission to the Yale R.O.T.C. The allocation to Freshmen of 100 places in the set total of 220 reflected the long-range military plan and preference for spreading the training in Field Artillery over the normal four-year college course, and otherwise safeguarding the interests of the general undergraduate curriculum. Student support of the new proposal was enthusiastic and contagious. Presently the campus swarmed with an eager army of applicants, waylaying members of the faculty for letters of recommendation and besieging the recruiting office of the Field Artillery Unit.

Day after day, the *Yale News* bore witness to the rapid march of kindred events. The College Student Council went on record as unanimously endorsing the idea of universal military training. On January 19, the results of a general undergraduate poll showed nearly four-fifths (1,112 to 288) of the voters in favor of universal military service. In these and like issues, national and local, the *News* was the chief exponent and advocate of progressive measures. Within a fortnight the organization of the Yale R.O.T.C. was practically completed. On February 8, the opening day of the second semester, the 220 men selected for the Training Unit began regular drilling in the work of Field Artillery.

In mid-February, plans for a Yale Naval Training Unit were rapidly matured. On February 26, the *News* carried the official announcement to the student body. More than 300 students promptly volunteered for this training, while a number of specially qualified faculty members such as Professors Abbott and Seward (who later became an honorary member of Torch) proffered their services as instructors. Progress was so encouraging that Rear Admiral Bradley E. Fiske strongly endorsed the project in a *Yale News* interview published on March 7: "I think the new Yale Naval Unit is a fine thing, the finest thing that any college has done since the present crisis faced us." With the firm establishment of Yale's two largest training units—the Yale R.O.T.C. in Field Artillery and the Yale Naval Training Unit—Yale University had, in reality, reached "the point of no return."

The First Yale Naval Aviation Unit

The quickened pace of Yale's preparation for the contingencies of war had other signal manifestations, notably in the novel and challenging field of aviation. Here, from the start, undergraduate initiative and determination had counted uncommonly. Under the lead of Trubee Davison, 1918, a group of twelve Yale students, mostly Yale College Juniors, had been organized and trained at Locust Valley, Long Island, during the summer of 1916 as the First Yale Naval Aviation Unit, and in September had taken part in Naval maneuvers off Sandy Hook, and later at the submarine base at New London. When, with expanding equipment and facilities, the initial group of twelve was correspondingly enlarged, one of the Torch founders, Graham Brush, became the first and only Sheff Senior in the membership of the Naval Aviation Unit, while one of the Torch Juniors, Kenneth Smith, likewise became a Sheff representative in the Unit. Another Torch Senior, Cord Meyer, whose early training in flying was already pointing him towards a commission in the Signal Corps of the Air Service, was among the Yale leaders in the general field of aviation.

On January 13, 1917, the *Yale News* fully reported and warmly endorsed the organization of the Yale Aero Club as a central means of advancing student interest in practical and scientific training in flying. The list of ten charter members, was headed by the following officers: Trubee Davison, 1918, President; Cord Meyer, 1917 S., Vice-President; Graham Brush, 1917 S., Secretary. The date of the announcement, which precisely coincided with the founding of the Yale R.O.T.C., emphasized the readiness and resourcefulness of student response to the changing conditions of the new year. To those who were considering the advent of Torch solely in its peace-time aspects, the prompt identification of two of its founders and one of its newly elected Juniors with the winter-term developments in aviation gave ready instances of constructive service to the growing needs of war-preparedness.

In early February, the final severance of diplomatic relations with Germany radically altered the national outlook and accelerated American military measures. On March 24, in full accord with the proposal of the Navy Department, the members of the First Yale Naval Aviation Unit enlisted in the Naval Reserve Force and, on March 28, left college for intensive training at West Palm Beach, Florida. Their sudden exodus as a body dramatized vividly the imminent threats of war. Within the Torch circle, the departure of Graham Brush and Kenneth Smith with the Yale Unit signalized the first pre-War inroads on the hitherto unbroken ranks of Torch. Beyond the immediate local impacts of the First Yale Naval Aviation Unit, its enduring influence was later attested by independent and supreme authority. Admiral Sims, in his book *Victory at Sea,* declared: "The great aircraft force which was ultimately assembled in Europe had its beginning in a small group of undergraduates at Yale University."

Alike by the University's official acts and by progressive undergraduate actions, the opening months of 1917 demonstrated conclusively the character of Yale's response to imperative national issues and needs. In the special fields of Field Artillery and Naval Aviation, Yale continued to lead the way, and in March became a recognized leader in the general field of Naval Training.

Other Aspects of the Winter Term

The national issues that quickened the pace of Yale's military preparations wrought gradual rather than revolutionary changes in the local scene and outlook. The carefully restricted numbers of the Field Artillery, Naval Aviation, and Naval Training Units comprised, during the winter term, less than a fifth of the entire undergraduate body. Under the long-range R.O.T.C. plan, the set total of 220 was made up of 100 Freshmen, 60 Sophomores, and 60 Juniors. "Seniors [it was expressly stated] will not be allowed to participate, but will be given an opportunity to receive coaching for the Federal examinations this spring for Reserve Officers' Commissions"—a provision that promised little save to Seniors who (like Sam Atkins, to cite a Torch example) had served with the Yale Batteries during the previous summer. Sheff upper-classmen found added restrictions inherent in the three-year Sheff system, with its mainly prescribed curriculum and heavy schedules. In further contrast with Yale College, Sheff made at first no allowance of credit hours towards a Yale degree to compensate for the extra work of the R.O.T.C. Thus few Sheff upper-classmen were free to undertake the combined programs of scholastic and military training. Even under the freer elective system of Yale College and the preferential plan of R.O.T.C. enrollments, the total number of Academic students in the various winter-term training units included only a relatively limited proportion of the whole College. Under such conditions regular curriculum and extra-curriculum activities were steadily maintained throughout the winter term.

New York "Victory Session"

Hardly had the *Yale News* and the *Yale Alumni Weekly* jointly heralded the advent of the Torch Honor Society when their columns emphasized a closely related event of unusual interest to Yale alumni and undergraduates. On Friday, January 19, 1917, several hundred former "Y" men, widely representing the four then recognized major sports, united in giving at the New York

Yale Club a testimonial dinner in honor of Captain Black and his championship team. Of the twelve men who had won the first Yale football victory over Harvard in nearly a decade, four were members of Torch—Black, LaRoche, Callahan, and Comerford —while a fifth Torch member (Carey) had played against Princeton, and a sixth (Bingham) had been a Varsity regular till invalided just before the Princeton and Harvard games. The Torch representation included nearly all Sheff members of the Varsity eleven—a concentration without campus precedent. Directly and impressively, the New York Victory Session associated the new Sheff Honor Society with outstanding leadership and service in Yale athletics. Against novel and dramatic backgrounds, the close coincidence of the advent of Torch with its quick launching into the main stream of current Yale activities and alumni interests stood forth strikingly. In the rapidly enlarging history of Torch, the mid-January meeting in New York marked a direct and far-reaching introduction to the company of alumni leaders and followers of Yale athletics. Vividly and vitally, it linked the newly launched undergraduate society not merely with the immediate fortunes of Yale football but with the enduring traditions of Yale athletic history.

Torch in Athletic Policy and Practice

As the winter term progressed, other indirect factors steadily identified Torch with the general athletic interests of the University. As the sole Sheff undergraduate member of the Yale Corporation's recently created Board of Control of Yale Athletics, Eddie Winters proved an active and influential representative. In early February he was appointed as the student member of the Board's special committee of five "to consider the question of providing in undergraduate recitation schedules a free period in the afternoon for athletics"—a problem especially acute in the congested Sheff programs. In early March he presented the report of another important special committee, "appointed to draw up By-Laws governing General Athletics." The detailed code submitted was thereupon ratified by the Board. Since "General

Athletics" covered all save the four established major sports, and since the new By-Laws advanced hockey and basket-ball mainly, if not fully, to the status of major sports, the scope and influence of the new code were uncommonly significant. Such constructive undergraduate aid helped to develop not alone the Board's new definitions of athletic policy and practice but the all-important spirit of mutual understanding and confidence between its alumni, student, and faculty members.

Within the general framework set up by the University's Board of Control, the practical administration of undergraduate athletic interests rested essentially with the Undergraduate Athletic Association, officially represented by its committee of ten, consisting of the captains and managers of the four major sports, together with two elected representatives of minor sports. In the 1917 committee, four of its eight *ex-officio* members were from Sheff. All four were Torch Seniors—captains Black and Meyer (football and crew), and managers Winters and Armstrong (baseball and crew). Chairman of the committee and president of the Undergraduate Athletic Association was Cord Meyer. Such comprehensive service to the common concerns of both Undergraduate Schools counted steadily in the firm maintenance of Yale athletics throughout the term, and in Academic as well as Sheff recognition of the range and continuity of the Torch contribution.

Sheff Senior Class Votes

In March, the Class of 1917 S. elected Farley Hopkins as its Class Orator, and in its official poll of class opinion and preferences gave leading honors to other Torch Seniors. On March 28, under the caption "Sheff Seniors Decide Black has Done Most for Yale," the *Yale News* opened its detailed review of the results of the Sheff Class Book committee's questionnaire, as follows:

According to the recently compiled statistics of the Senior class of the Scientific School, C. R. Black, Jr., Captain of last fall's championship football team, has done most for Yale. He was also voted the most popular, the best natured, and the most loyal man in his class. G. M.

Brush, of Greenwich, Conn., who has gone to Florida with the Naval
Aerial Unit, was voted the most likely to succeed.

In the accompanying numerical statistics, it was recorded that the
vote for Black as the man who had done most for Yale was
"unanimous." Besides this unique distinction, he was decisively
chosen as the man who had "done most for Sheff." Of the four
others named in this latter vote, two were founders of Torch—
Graham Brush and Sam Atkins. Another of the founders, Roy
Crawford, a high-ranking honor student, was the emphatic choice
of the class as its "most scholarly" representative. In previous
elections he had been chosen as class treasurer and as president of
the Student Council. Such independent and tangible evidence of
the consensus of Senior class opinion was naturally reassuring to
the group of classmates who had pointed the Torch project
towards its central aim of constructive service to the University
and to Sheff. To this recognition of distinctive contributions to
the familiar interests of peace were immediately added fresh
proofs of influential Torch coöperation in the challenging concerns of war.

The Advent and Declaration of War

In late March and early April, 1917, the mounting tide of national
commitments to the Allied cause rose to full height. In the Yale
calendar it coincided with the closing week of the winter term and
the opening days of the spring vacation. On March 28, ten days
before the Declaration of War by the United States, the "First
Official Yale University War Memorandum on the Attitude of
the University in the Present Crisis," was issued over the signatures of the leading officers of Yale, and widely published next
day in the public press. Its impressive scope and precise detail
made it forthwith the charter of Yale's attitude and official actions.
The response of undergraduate Yale was instant and invigorating.
Within a few hours its representative athletic committee, with
whose activities and leadership Torch was so closely identified,
took characteristic action. In its next issue (March 29), the *Yale*

News fully reported and endorsed the results of this special meeting. The opening paragraphs of the official report of the committee of ten are indicative:

At a meeting of the Undergraduate Committee of the Athletic Association yesterday morning it was voted "That all intercollegiate athletics be cancelled within twenty-four hours after a declaration of war by the United States Government." This measure is in direct accord with the statement, published in yesterday's NEWS by the University officials, but it was thought advisable for the Undergraduate Committee of the Athletic Association to take action in the matter in view of the uncertainty in many minds as to just how athletics would be affected by such a declaration—particularly in the Easter vacation.

A further purpose was to obtain some definite basis upon which arrangements may be made with other teams. The crew, for instance, has a race with Pennsylvania in the Easter vacation, and it seems now unnecessary to cancel it. If, however, war should be declared during the vacation, it would be possible in this way for both crews either to know at once that the race was cancelled, or else to make arrangements to row it within twenty-four hours.

Equally practical provisions covered the existing schedule of daily games of the baseball team on its usual southern trip during the spring vacation, and assured its prompt abandonment in the event of war.

An accompanying *News* editorial, entitled "War and Athletics," declared that the action of the committee "is significant of the fact that the students approve absolutely of the authorities' wish, expressed in the official statement yesterday. . . . This vote, coming as it does from a group of undergraduates who have thought carefully upon the subject, is indicative of the feeling of respect which the students hold for the judgment of the University officials in the present state of affairs." The forthright action of the committee of ten, which thus exemplified the force of thoughtful student coöperation, was all the more influential since the campus was well aware that the captains and managers of crew and baseball, the two Varsity sports most immediately affected, were participants in the crucial decisions. Within the next ten days the foresight and efficacy of such undergraduate leadership were to be demonstrated conclusively.

The first week of April marked the American entrance into the European War. On Monday, April 2, President Wilson delivered his historic Address to Congress calling for the Declaration of War against Germany. The successive actions of both branches of Congress were officially implemented on Friday, April 6, by the President's Proclamation of the State of War. On the preceding Wednesday, Yale had closed for the usual week of the Easter recess, and the baseball team had departed for its regular southern trip, and the two Varsity crews for Philadelphia for practice before the scheduled races with the University of Pennsylvania on Saturday, April 7. In ready accord with the specific provisions of the Yale Athletic Association, Yale's intercollegiate program came to an end with the mid-vacation contests of Saturday.

The brief, but completely successful, seasons of the Yale nine and crews had a dramatic ending. With its final victory over the University of North Carolina the undefeated baseball team concluded a striking record. That same afternoon, on the Schuylkill River, both Yale crews won their races by spectacular finishes. Torch representation alike in Varsity baseball and rowing was active and characteristic. Both managers—Eddie Winters and Chauncey Armstrong—were Torch founders, as were Cord Meyer, who captained the two crews, and Sam Atkins who, together with Arthur Page, one of the Torch Juniors, rowed in the first boat. On the nine, Ed Munson was the regular catcher, and Charlie Comerford and Bob Carey were among the leading pitchers. In the dramatic fulfillment, as in the determination, of Yale athletic policy, the joint events of April 7 were doubly significant. To the instant and insistent reconciliation of the demands of peace and war Torch made significant contribution. In the external history of the Torch Honor Society, Saturday, April 7, 1917 marks the dramatic conclusion of the first eventful chapter of its peace-time services and the opening of a new chapter to be determined in terms of war.

Internal Developments in Torch

The winter term of 1917 which established Torch in manifold active relations to University and undergraduate affairs was also a fortunate period in the Society's internal development. To safeguard against the contingencies of war, Torch had advanced the time of its Junior class elections to December, 1916, in bold departure from the traditions of May Senior Society (and Aurelian) elections. The long winter months that intervened before the April 6 Declaration of War gave the incoming Juniors unusual time to familiarize themselves with the aims and standards of their predecessors. They found the energy, loyalty, and spirit of teamplay of the Torch founders infectious. They themselves were men of action and achievement to whom the Torch conception of vigorous and concerted Yale service appealed instinctively. In the stimulating comradeship of Torch they found fresh incentives to individual and group endeavor. In turn, they imparted to the Society new resources of vital energy and enthusiasm.

The Wall Street Headquarters

The winter-term meetings of Torch, regularly held on Tuesday evenings, took place in unpretentious but readily accessible quarters on Wall Street, just below York Hall. Round the corner was St. Anthony Hall, 133 College Street. Down Wall Street, on its south side, stretched a block of dwellings mainly occupied as Sheff lodging-houses. In one of them (that of Mrs. Peters) Torch rented the meeting-room which provided, for the first time, a definite center in the midst of "Shefftown."

This first home of Torch was sparsely furnished. Its initial outfit was limited to a few tables, a rug or two, and a scant supply of chairs. These latter were presently supplemented with the "six blue over-stuffed chairs" of cherished memory, whose recovery after the War represented the survival of the fittest of these early material possessions. On the walls of the meeting-room, however, hung the framed document of the Founders' joint agreement of 1916 and the Torch plaque—the enduring symbols of the origin and spiritual inheritance of Torch.

With the added numbers of the incoming Junior delegation, the Torch quarters barely sufficed. The Spartan simplicity of the Wall Street meeting-place was in odd contrast with the comforts of the spacious chapter-houses and well-appointed halls to which the Torch members had been long accustomed in their various Sheff societies and fraternities. The very proximity of the Sheff Society buildings close at hand might, indeed, have invited ironic reminders that while, with Torch, austerity was the inevitable order of the day, prosperity lay just round the Wall Street corner. In the resolute philosophy of the Torch founders, happily, there was neither room nor need for envious comparisons. Had they needed a reassuring text they might have taken it from Bacon's *Essays* (then currently included in the curriculum of the "Select Course" in Sheff): "Prosperity is not without many fears and distastes; and adversity is not without comforts and hopes."

Torch Faculty Members

In reviewing the internal history of Torch during the winter term of 1917, its central development as an undergraduate society remains characteristic. In contrast with Aurelian, with its many faculty and alumni honorary members, the campus viewed and judged Torch solely in its undergraduate aspects, first disclosed in the December, 1916 announcements of its student membership. Neither then nor later in the academic year was there indication of faculty connections. The personal consultations with Professors Roe and Schreiber that had brought them into close and confidential relations with the Senior group never needed formal definition. The threatening external conditions that had led Torch to concentrate on early election of the ten Juniors from the Class of 1918 S. had no such urgent bearings on questions of faculty contacts. Nevertheless, with the doubled numbers and strength of undergraduate representation, the status and possible increase of faculty affiliations within the Torch circle were definitely reconsidered.

Under the growing uncertainties of the national and local situation Torch entertained no thoughts of entering the general field of honorary alumni elections or of greatly expanding its special faculty connections. It was, however, decided to consult a third member of the Sheff faculty and at the same time to invite him to join the Society as an "honorary member." This first adoption by Torch of a term in current campus use set up a convenient category of membership, but it was a distinction without a difference in the communal life of the Society.

The new "honorary member," Professor George H. Nettleton, a Yale College graduate of 1896, had joined the Sheff faculty in 1898 as instructor in English, and in 1916, upon the appointment of Professor Wilbur L. Cross as Dean of the Graduate School, had succeeded him as head of the Sheff English Department. Meanwhile, other posts of service as division officer of the Select Course, as Senior Class officer, and as Sheff faculty representative on the recently named Board of Control of Yale Athletics, had connected him with Sheff and general undergraduate interests. With the enrollment of its third Sheff faculty member and of its full Senior and Junior quotas, Torch completed and consolidated its membership for the winter term of 1917. Throughout that term the three faculty associates shared intimately in the councils and fellowship of Torch and steadily supported its central development as an undergraduate society.

The Torch "Criticisms"

Once installed in their winter quarters, the combined Torch groups settled down promptly to study questions that had been intentionally left open till the incoming Juniors could share in solving them. Among such pending questions was one of deep import to the thought and inner life of the new Honor Society. In their October conferences with Professor Roe, the Torch Seniors had approved, in principle, a major proposal which he had initiated and gradually shaped into the plan familiarly known to the Torch founders and to their successors as the *Criticisms*. The problem now was to implement the aims vividly recalled in Graham Brush's detailed review of the October conferences. (Previously quoted in full, pp. 16–17.) In his own words, "What we later called 'Criticisms' was the mechanism or means by which the members could learn to know one another so thoroughly as to bind the group into a solid unit." Though the scope and penetration of such definition were but imperfectly reflected in the term *Criticisms,* its convenience gave it ready and persistent currency in the Torch vocabulary. If the word never fully suited the proposed action or its proponents there was no mistaking of the constructive purposes of the *Criticisms.*

From the outset, the Torch founders had linked with their primary aim of constructive Yale service the kindred aim of "developing men for leadership in college and in after life." It was to this special end that the *Criticisms* sought to contribute. They offered the individual member added means of thoughtful self-expression and self-development, and deepened within the Society the sense of mutual understanding and endeavor. Since the plan was intended to apply broadly to successive Senior groups as class units, the general framework was kept simple. In its salient aspects it combined the methods of interpretative autobiography and of group discussion. It applied to the personal interests and problems of the active undergraduate members the constructive spirit characteristic of the Torch discussions of Yale interests and problems.

Viewed independently, the new plan had two essential elements: (1) personal histories or "Autobiographies," reviewing the events and influences that had mainly led the individual to enter college and had shaped his immediate objectives in Sheff and his outlook towards the concerns of later life; and (2) group discussions or "Criticisms," based on the content and qualities of the given "Autobiographies." Within this general frame of reference, the individual participants were left free to determine the best ways to make their own contributions meaningful to themselves and to their associates. Such freedom of thought and utterance was implicit in a plan that tested the judgment and encouraged the resourcefulness of the individual. Such constraints as it involved were virtually self-imposed. In minimizing the machinery of the new project, the Torch reaffirmed its faith in the spirit of its active interpreters.

The new Torch plan offered no such ready criteria of judgment as were familiar in the case of extra-curriculum activities. Its service lay not in that outer world of activity but in the inner world of intensive thought. Its conception of individual development involved deliberate reflection and judgment on more than momentary issues. Its objectives may be clarified in the light of an independent, but suggestive, event in the pre-War experience of Sheff. In 1908, Leet Oliver Hall had been given as a memorial of Daniel Leet Oliver, who had died after the close of the Junior year of the Class of 1908 S. In September, 1908, the new Sheff building had been opened as a center for the teaching of the cultural studies—English, history, and social sciences—especially emphasized in the Select Course, in which Lêet Oliver had been enrolled. On a granite scroll above the Hillhouse Avenue entrance to the Memorial Hall were inscribed lines chosen to dedicate its classrooms to the culture of liberal studies in the Scientific School. Taken from the poem in which Tennyson interprets the classic story of the conflicting choices and rewards of life which the rival goddesses offered to the youthful Paris, the lines voice the probing counsel of the Goddess of Wisdom:

> Self-reverence, self-knowledge, self-control:
> These three alone lead life to sovereign power.

In like spirit, the new Torch plan interpreted the worth of training in the humanities of life and learning.

The project of the Torch *Criticisms,* which had been approved in principle in October, 1916, was unanimously adopted in late February, 1917, as defined by the progressive discussions of the winter months. It had been conceived and developed in terms of the normal conditions in times of peace. Now, under the mounting threats of war, it became evident that there was scant time for testing its practical efficacy. Nevertheless, prior to the Declaration of War and the general dispersal of Torch members to the Officers' Training Camps, such actual tests were initiated with encouraging results. The stress of the Torch *Criticisms* on the qualities of disciplined service and leadership took on heightened meaning in the confronting issues of war. Thus, before the end of the winter term of 1917, the *Criticisms* became a vital part of the organic structure and life of Torch. When, at the close of World War I, the Society faced the crucial tests of reintegration, the demonstrated strength of the *Criticisms* proved a renewing force in the re-dedication of the Torch enterprise to the services of peace.

The Aurelian Manifesto of March 7, 1917

On March 7, 1917, the Aurelian Honor Society published in the *Yale News* a carefully detailed official statement of its "standards and qualifications" for undergraduate membership. It was appended to its announcement of the election of three additional members from the Class of 1917 S., thus bringing the number of its active Seniors to *ten*. Further action before the end of Senior year was plainly indicated: "There are two more Seniors eligible before May 15, 1917." These present and prospective steps were of special interest to the members of Torch since their own December elections had established the "First Ten" as the basic unit for Junior class representation, and at the same time, by the addition of two more Seniors, had enlarged the 1917 S. delegation to *twelve*—precisely the number which Aurelian now proposed to reach in "the final election before the end of Senior year." Besides these numerical coincidences, the Torch members found the March Aurelian elections an interesting departure from the previous Aurelian policy of deferring all additional Senior elections till the class was about to graduate. The general trend of these various steps was in the direction already pointed in the December Torch elections. The enlargement of the basic Junior unit to ten and the early incorporation of the additional Seniors into the active class membership, essential elements in the original Torch project, and now openly influential, were to become after the War permanently established factors in the policy and practice of both Honor Societies.

The extensive Aurelian statement appended to its announcement of March elections had like significance as its first official manifesto issued since the founding of Torch. Its full text read thus:

Owing to the fact that in past years the influence of the Aurelian Honor Society in promoting the welfare of the Sheffield Scientific School has been somewhat curtailed by confusion arising from ignorance of the Society's standards and qualifications, it wishes to dispel any misunderstanding regarding these standards and qualifications by publishing them in explicit and concrete form. The Aurelian Society is of the opinion that if an honor society is to encourage and stimulate high ideals and distinguished attainments in the undergraduate body, it can best provide an incentive by announcing its aims and principles.

The Aurelian Honor Society was founded to recognize present ability, high moral character, gentlemanly conduct, and the promise of future achievements, in the undergraduates of the Sheffield Scientific School, and to promote the application of these qualities to the service of the community.

Election to the Society is based upon the following requirements: 1. A minimum average scholarship standing of 65 per cent., i.e., 2.60 [on the scale of 4.00], at the time of election shall be required. 2. A man shall be valued according to: (1) moral, personal, and mental characteristics; (2) gentlemanly conduct; (3) position as evidenced by the respect of the class; (4) promise of future achievement, and (5) general intellectual ability.

The most representative man in each of the following arts shall be taken who fulfills best the above mentioned qualifications, scientific, literary, oratorical, executive, educational, religious, and athletic. Not more than two men may be taken under one classification until the final election before the end of the Senior year. There are two more Seniors eligible before May 15, 1917.

That so open and so prominent a manifesto attracted no independent *Yale News* comment or communications was in no wise surprising. Especially since the final severance in February of diplomatic relations with Germany, national issues had overshadowed local concerns. The campus was content to leave to their own devices the Sheff and College societies now faced by emergent problems. Certainly Torch encountered no pressure to match the Aurelian statement. Within the Torch circle, where anticipation of the contingencies of war had long influenced thought and action, it was strongly felt that the times were ill-suited to controversial debate involving the many details of the peace-time concerns and procedures of the Sheff Honor Societies. This feeling was soon accentuated by the departure of two of its members—Graham Brush and Ken Smith—with the First Yale Naval Aviation Unit for intensive training at West Palm Beach, Florida. This first dramatic exodus from the Yale campus signalized to the entire undergraduate body the reality of Yale response to the call to the colors.

The Close of the Winter Term

During the final week of the winter term, the University's First Official War Memorandum published on March 28 was the greatest common factor in undergraduate thought and action. Its contagious influence, already instanced in the supporting actions of the Undergraduate Athletic Association and of the *Yale News,* was equally evident in other measures of prompt readjustment to new conditions. Day after day, in quick succession, the various Sheff societies and fraternities announced their lists of Freshman elections normally given in May. On March 31 appeared the Aurelian list, which included the two additional Seniors and the seven Juniors that completed quotas usually filled in mid-May. In Yale College, the Senior Societies advanced the date of Tap Day to April 19.

At the *Yale News* dinner on March 30 the response of the entire Yale community to the Yale War Memorandum was strikingly voiced by the undergraduate and faculty speakers, and eloquently commended by President Hadley. On April 1, a patriotic rally of Town and Gown crowded Woolsey Hall to its doors. In the scholastic field, the new Elective Pamphlet stressed the addition of military training as the fourth grand division in the course of study. At the same time the preliminary canvass for a greatly enlarged R.O.T.C. showed convincing student demand. In every phase of campus activities and of the University's new war program the spirit of undergraduate support was heartening. The winter term closed with the local stage set for the impending drama of war.

CHAPTER IV

THE SPRING TERM OF 1917

ON APRIL 12, 1917, following the Easter recess made momentous by the American Declaration of War, Yale reopened. The returning Torch undergraduates, who had long anticipated the present crisis, found the acquired experience of their past three months invaluable. Though two Torch members were now in Florida in active training with the First Yale Naval Aviation Unit, the foresight and initiative of the December Torch elections had provided complete Senior and Junior groups and had consolidated their numbers. Such early and independent action had now become doubly significant in the light of the hurriedly advanced elections of the other Sheff societies in late March. During the vacation, the many connections of Torch with Yale athletics had been newly demonstrated in the strength of Torch representation in the membership, leadership, and undergraduate management of the victorious Varsity crews and baseball team. As the new term opened, the return of the eight Torch members thus directly associated with the successful conclusion of Yale's athletic program and with immediate adjustment to the University's new war-time policy reaffirmed the spirit and service of Torch under the sudden tests of war emergencies.

The April War Program

On April 11, the University Emergency Council issued its Second Official War Memorandum, defining the course of action to be followed during the coming term. In voicing "its conviction that the most important military service which the University can render at this time is the training of artillery officers through the Reserve Officers' Training Corps," the Emergency Council announced plans for the rapid expansion of the Yale R.O.T.C. and for "daily military drill open both to students and members of the Faculty."

With the opening of the spring term on Thursday, April 12,

the new program was quickly launched. That afternoon, at a University Mass Meeting in Woolsey Hall, Captain Danford explained the detailed provisions for military drill and instruction and the methods of application for enrollment. Student response was enthusiastic. On Friday afternoon some 1,270 volunteers for the R.O.T.C. reported at the Muster held on the Old Campus and were thereupon organized into more than 30 platoons. On Monday morning still larger numbers joined in inaugurating the general "setting-up exercises under the direction of Captain Danford to be held on the College Campus every week-day morning from 7.00 to 7.30," and "recommended to all students in the University." Various provisions of the University Emergency Council likewise furthered the rapid expansion of the Yale Naval Training Unit and other means of war training.

The Response of Torch

Torch participation in the new program was eager and widespread. The substantial nucleus of members already identified with aviation, field artillery, and naval training soon grew to include most of the Juniors, as well as the Seniors. The April 14 announcement that Sheff men enlisting in the R.O.T.C. would henceforth share with Yale College students in the set allowance of scholastic credit for military training opened entrances hitherto blocked by heavy schedule requirements. Later in the term, when a recruiting officer of the U.S. Marine Corps invited the Dean of the College and the Director of the Scientific School to recommend ten outstanding undergraduates for commissions, they were equally divided between the two Schools. One of the Sheff appointees was Edward J. Winters, who was duly commissioned Second Lieutenant in the Marine Corps in May. Cord Meyer, early commissioned First Lieutenant in the Air Service, became in mid-July one of its first officers engaged in overseas service. In April, Clinton Black and Farley Hopkins enrolled in the U.S. Naval Reserve Force. The spirit of unity in diversity of service which had animated the Torch pioneers in times of peace remained characteristic in the emergencies of war.

Tap Day and its Aftermath

On Thursday, April 19, Tap Day—held simultaneously at Palm Beach and New Haven—brought home dramatically to a khaki-clad campus the force of unprecedented changes. This first Yale College Tap Day since the founding of Torch was deeply meaningful to the new Sheff Honor Society. It climaxed the movement of all undergraduate Yale societies towards war-accelerated elections and readjustments which Torch had set in train months ago. The Tap Day elections given in Florida to some dozen Yale College Juniors in active training with the First Yale Naval Aviation Unit were of added interest to Torch through the presence of the two Torch members in that Unit. The linking ceremonies at Palm Beach and on the College Campus gave, not alone to the College but to Sheff, dramatic reminders of the pre-War departure of the Yale Unit which had forecast the general exodus from the campus of Yale upper-classmen now imminent.

The week-end after Tap Day quickened the pace of campus readjustment to war conditions. The Friday issue of the *Yale News* which published the lists of Senior Society elections announced the plans of the War Department for a nation-wide system of military camps for the training of U.S. Army officers to be opened in early May. The response of Yale volunteers was instant and incisive. On Saturday, the *News* carried an arresting caption: "Two Hundred Men Sign Up for First Military Camps." By Monday the number had risen to nearly 500. Such testimony was the more impressive since few save upper-classmen could meet the set age requirement. The *News* had a suggestive comment:

> Twenty years and nine months has been officially set as the minimum age limit for admission to the Reserve Officers Training Camps. Automatically two-thirds of the men now enrolled in the present Yale military units are thus debarred from acceptance at these camps.

To the majority of qualified upper-classmen of both Undergraduate Schools, however, admittance to the May Training Camps became their primary concern. The stimulus of the Army plans was further felt in different Yale units in process of formation. On April 26 the *News* announced that "the first Yale Unit of the American Ambulance serving in France is being formed to go to France in June." The plans of the Yale Naval Unit advanced apace. Special services, such as the Marine Corps, developed likewise. The stir of student response was omnipresent.

The Militant March of Torch

Within the Torch circle the import of the main trend to the May Training Camps was keenly sensed. Already the departure of Graham Brush and Ken Smith with the First Yale Naval Aviation Unit and the commitment of other Torch members to different branches of war service had given direct foretastes of the general exodus now close at hand. Upon the announcement of the Army plans, most Torch Seniors not otherwise involved volunteered at once for the May Training Camps, as the first step towards gaining commissions in Field Artillery. Individual variants from this general pattern still continued. Farley Hopkins, who enrolled on April 22 as boatswain's mate in the U.S. Naval Reserve Force, was presently assigned to a boat which he had helped to provide for special service. The *Yale News* of May 2 added details:

A submarine chaser has been bought by Farley Hopkins, 1917 S. and Dwight Wiman, 1918 S. The boat is 105 feet in length and develops a speed of 20 knots per hour. The base of the *Alcada* for the present is the Brooklyn Navy Yard. The boat has a cruising radius of 700 miles. The crew will consist of fourteen Yale men and four from the regular Navy.

Closely linked with Farley Hopkins was his Torch classmate, Anthony Bullock, who enlisted on May 8 in the Naval Reserve and was likewise assigned to the *Alcada*. Even with the Army's deferment of the opening date of the Training Camps from May 8 to May 14, and with the continuance in the Yale R.O.T.C. of some of the Torch Juniors, it was clear that, within a few weeks, at most, Torch representation on the campus would be drastically reduced.

The general Torch outlook was further clarified when the first Torch Senior applicants for the First Military Training Camps received official notification of their acceptance and of their individual assignments to the designated camps, chiefly in the Eastern area. Looking beyond the May foregrounds the Torch group could visualize the September prospect of undergraduate membership reduced to a very few of the present Juniors. In the fortifying experience of Torch during the past months there had been no wavering between the issues of war and peace, no inconstancies in reinterpreting the spirit of active service to University interests in terms of militant national service. By mid-May the Yale campus became, for the Torch, not the center of its normal activities but the point of common departure for widely distributed fields of intensive training. The closing of the Society's winter headquarters on Wall Street was in itself a silent token that Torch had enlisted for the duration of the War.

The Central Service of the Yale R.O.T.C.

The opening month of the spring term that dominantly transformed the undergraduate campus into a Campus Martius had its factors of stability as well as of change. Successive War Memoranda of the University Emergency Council steadily counselled most students "below the age for Officers' Training Camps . . . to go on with their school courses and with their regular college or professional work, especially if the latter be in such departments as medicine, chemistry, or engineering, where the demand for thoroughly trained men is pressing and sure to continue. . . . The need now is not so much for hasty and haphazard attempts by each individual to get as quickly as possible to the firing line, as for quiet, determined and conscientious preparation to meet the Government's demands when clearly formulated and enforced."

A second and most potent factor of stability lay in the Yale R.O.T.C., with its established tradition of effective training in Field Artillery. From the outset of the spring term, the wide expansion and firm organization of the Yale Unit, and its correlation with the work of the regular undergraduate curriculum, had offered exceptional opportunities to fulfill the double demands of scholastic and military preparation for war service. The opening, on April 23, of the Evening School of Military Instruction, led by Captain Danford and largely taught by qualified members of the Faculty, was another integrating factor in the required work of all platoons of the R.O.T.C. development. On May 14, following the departure of upper-classmen accepted for the first Officers' Training Camps, Captain Danford, in his impressive address to the remaining student body, gave reassuring counsel:

I feel strongly that it is most inadvisable for the younger men to leave college now. They should not join anything which will prevent their returning to the University next fall. College men at present too young will be seriously needed later as officers. The college man should enter the field where he can best render service, and that is conceded to be as a commissioned officer.

Like local developments and like perspectives, as evident in the long-range plans of the Yale Naval Unit, further focused student attention on the emphasized needs of thorough basic preparation for a war of long duration.

Torch Juniors and Sheff Concerns

While the May exodus from the campus of most Seniors and many Juniors was the chief centrifugal force in immediate Yale experience, the stabilizing factors in the local scene were widely influential in the remaining student body. In Sheff the spring term transfers of office from Senior to Junior hands progressed much as usual. On April 26, the Sheff Interfraternity Council announced its chosen members for the next year. Three of the eight appointees were Torch Juniors—Alvan Macauley, Edwin Munson, and Northam Wright. On May 4, the Byers Hall Y.M.C.A. (the Sheff counterpart to Dwight Hall in Yale College) chose Tom Crawford and Alvan Macauley, both Torch Juniors, as President and as Vice-President. On May 8, the Junior class chose Chester ("Chet") LaRoche, chairman of the 1918 S. Torch delegation, as Chairman of the Sheff Senior Council for 1918. On June 4, the *Yale News* announced the formation of an Undergraduate Emergency Council "with the primary purpose of campaigning the University for Liberty Loan Bonds." Among the Sheff representatives on this joint Council were Tom Crawford and Alvan Macauley. Such appointments to posts of leadership in Sheff affairs and of service to the common interests reflected the independent judgment of the undergraduate community.

Under rapidly changing war conditions Sheff elections to office for the coming year were naturally subject to successive changes as individual withdrawals from college for active war service increased. On May 22, Chet LaRoche enrolled in the U.S. Naval Reserve Force, was commissioned Ensign on June 28, and sent to Annapolis in the Navy's first war class. To fill the vacancy thus created, Tom Crawford was elected as Chairman of the Sheff Senior Council for 1918. When, in the course of his Senior year, he enlisted in the U.S. Marine Corps (where he was later commissioned Second Lieutenant), he was followed in the Sheff chairmanship by Northam Wright. Such continuing turns of the Sheff kaleidoscope revealed not alone the compelling changes of war-times but constant campus reliance on the qualities of leadership manifest in the Junior Torch group.

Torch Seniors in the May Training Camps

The gradual exodus of Torch members, begun prior to the Declaration of War, became pronounced with the opening of the first Army Officers' Training Camps on May 14, 1917. Hitherto, especially with Torch Seniors, the diversity of early enlistments in various branches of war service had been strongly marked. Now the main emphasis fell on the May Training Camps as the readiest means towards attainment of commissions in the Field Artillery. Here the backgrounds of previous training under Captain Danford counted directly. Sam Atkins, who had served with the Yale Batteries in the summer of 1916 and later with the Yale R.O.T.C., entered the O.T.C. at Plattsburg and was commissioned Captain in Field Artillery on August 15. Other Torch Seniors at the same camp—Roy Crawford and Ed Munson—won their lieutenancies on the same day. At camps farther afield, Charles Sheldon at Fort

Riley, Kansas, and Wiley Krotzer at Fort Oglethorpe, Georgia, similarly won their lieutenancies on August 15.

The five Torch Seniors thus commissioned at the close of the first Officers' Training Camps were further linked since all later served actively in the foreign field, four as Captains, and one as First Lieutenant, in Field Artillery. In point of numerical distribution of the twelve members of the 1917 S. Torch group among various branches of war service, the five Field Artillery officers formed the largest contingent, followed by the three in the U.S. Naval Reserve Force, and the two in Aviation (one in the U.S. Naval Reserve Flying Corps, and one in the Air Corps), and single representatives in the Marine Corps and in the Ordnance Department. In the totality and breadth of such response to the challenge of war the Torch Seniors exemplified anew the spirit of unity in diversity of service that, from the outset, had animated the Torch enterprise.

Torch Juniors in War Service

The general dispersal of the Torch Seniors to war-training bases was accompanied by like departures from the 1918 group. Of the "First Ten" Juniors elected in December, 1916, the earliest to leave college was Kenneth Smith, who went to Florida with the First Yale Naval Aviation Unit in March, 1917. In September, as an officer of the U.S. Naval Reserve Flying Corps, attached to the French Aviation Forces, he began his long career of active service overseas, thrice signalized by the awards of the *Croix de Guerre,* the *Légion d'Honneur,* and the Navy Cross, "for distinguished and heroic service." Three of the Torch Juniors early enrolled in the U.S. Naval Reserve Force—Chet LaRoche and Tim Callahan in May, and Arthur Page in June, 1917—and later won commissions and promotions as Naval officers.

The chosen form of service of two other Juniors was Field Artillery. Harold ("Bill") Carey remained temporarily in the Yale R.O.T.C., pending his admission in August to the Second O.T.C. at Plattsburg, where on November 25 he was commissioned Captain, Field Artillery. Alvan Macauley, who continued in the Yale R.O.T.C. till the following June, was assigned immediately upon his Sheff graduation to Camp Jackson, South Carolina, where he received his lieutenancy in Field Artillery. Among the Juniors who left college early was Charlie Comerford, who entered war service in June, 1917, and began in the following February a year of foreign service, during which he was detached from the U.S. Army Medical Department for three months' training at the Artillery School at Saumur, France. On August 31 he was there commissioned Second Lieutenant in the U.S. Coast Artillery Corps, serving overseas thereafter with the 67th C.A.C.

As with the Torch Seniors, the wide distribution of the Juniors in different branches of war service was early and increasingly marked. In April, 1918, Tom Crawford enrolled in the Marine Corps, where he became a Second Lieutenant, while Northam Wright later entered the Army Medical Department and served at Camp Greenleaf, Georgia. In the range and inclusiveness of Torch participation in war activities, the Juniors vied with their Senior predecessors. In the progressive history of Torch during the spring term of 1917 the successive departures of the majority of the Juniors are all the more striking since special factors, such as the near approach of graduation and the May opening of the First Officers' Training Camps, which counted immediately in the decisions of-Seniors, had no such urgency in the case of Juniors.

The Concluding Weeks of the Spring Term

From the middle to the close of the spring term, the absence of the Seniors who had founded Torch and the dwindling of the Junior ranks were acutely felt by the few remaining Torch representatives on campus. Their own pre-occupation with local war training, especially in the Yale R.O.T.C. and in the Yale Naval Training Unit, and their personal services on Sheff committees (instanced in the section on "Torch Juniors and Sheff Concerns") were individual rather than group activities of Torch.

Under prevalent conditions, it was realized that it was no longer feasible to maintain the system of regular meetings that had developed the inner life of the Society. The plan of "Criticisms," evolved prior to the Declaration of War as a comprehensive group activity uniting all members of a Torch delegation, was set aside, for the time being, for lack of numbers and leisure. The crowded daytime schedules, beginning with the early morning half-hour of setting-up exercises on the campus and concluding with late afternoon military drills, the Evening School of Military Instruction with its requisites of preparatory study, and the prescribed courses of the Sheff curriculum were priorities that daily confronted the remnant of Torch Juniors. The three faculty members of Torch, variously engaged in added activities such as those of the Faculty Batteries of Field Artillery, the Evening School of Military Instruction, and the University's committee on the First Liberty Loan, had also their regular priorities of teaching and counselling in Sheff. Brief meetings of such Torch members, undergraduate and faculty, as proved available on the spur of the moment or of some war emergency inevitably replaced the deliberate discussions of Sheff and University affairs that, under normal conditions, had consistently shaped the internal development of the Society. Fortunately the strength of Torch lay not in numbers or conformity to custom but in the unbroken spirit of comradeship-in-arms. On May 12, Torch held its final meeting of the year to bid God-speed to those on the eve of departure for the mid-May camps.

During the closing weeks of the academic year, the Torch members still in college had significant reminders of their predecessors now widely dispersed in different fields of war training. The three Torch Seniors at the Plattsburg Camp were associated with the testimonial presented, on behalf of "the three hundred and more Yale men now at Plattsburg," to Captain Danford on the occasion of the memorable Yale dinner in his honor held in New York City on May 31. Pointed reminders of Torch connections with naval and aviation service followed. The June 1 issue of the *Yale Alumni Weekly* carried a characteristic picture showing "Ex-Captain Black of the Varsity Eleven Drilling a Company at Newport," at that Rhode Island Naval Base. The

June 15 issue had an announcement of direct interest to Torch: "The Yale Aerial Coast Patrol Unit No. 1, who have been training in Florida for the Naval Reserve Aero Corps, have been moved to Huntington, N.Y." For the two Torch representatives in that pioneer Yale Unit it marked a point of definite progress towards the goal of active service overseas. These and like reminders brought home vividly to the Society the realization that the paths of service, however divergent for the time being, were steadily converging towards the common goal. In that unifying faith and growing experience the Torch Honor Society carried forward.

The Yale Commencement of June, 1917

The Yale Commencement Week of June 17–20, 1917 brought to its dramatic ending a year of supreme decision and action. The program of Commencement events everywhere visualized and vitalized the dominant theme of patriotic service. On Tuesday afternoon, the traditional Harvard–Yale baseball game was replaced by the Dedication of the new Artillery Armory, given by alumni and erected near Yale Field. Instead of the colorful parades of reunion classes, the March to the Field was chiefly of detachments of various Yale units in active training. Olive drab and Navy blue dominated the local scene. The token flight of Navy planes from Huntington, Long Island, the new training base of the First Yale Naval Aviation Unit, to and above Yale Field lent an added touch. Following the ceremonies at Artillery Hall and the return to the campus came the stirring Patriotic Exercises where, from the balcony of Woolsey Hall overlooking the University Quadrangle, President Hadley, Captain Danford, and George E. Vincent, '85, addressed the Yale cohorts gathered below.

On Tuesday evening, the meetings of reunion classes were supplemented by a general dinner in the University Dining Hall for some 450 members of non-reunion classes. At this so-called "1492 Dinner" the speakers were Major-General Clarence R. Edwards, U.S.A., Commander of the Northeastern Department, stationed at Boston; George H. Nettleton, '96, of the Sheff faculty, recently appointed by the Yale Corporation as Director of the prospective Yale Bureau in Paris, designed as a center for Yale men in all forms of overseas service; and Frederic C. Walcott, '91, who for the past two years had been engaged in Belgian and Polish relief work.

On Wednesday morning, the crowning Commencement Exercises in Woolsey Hall deepened and heightened the import of the war-time Yale Commemoration. The number of undergraduate degrees conferred *in absentia* and the presence of many Seniors in uniform who received their diplomas in person were doubly significant. Short furloughs from Plattsburg, Newport, and other near-by training camps enabled a considerable number to rejoin their classmates for the Yale Graduation. The conferring of honorary degrees for distinguished service to the arts of peace and to the necessities of war carried the audience to fresh heights of enthusiasm and of inspiration. At the name of Robert Melville Danford, presented as the first of the recipients of honorary degrees, the whole assembly rose in contagious tribute, while the popular acclaim was redoubled as the citations of the Public Orator, Professor Woolsey, and of President Hadley made known to the Yale community the happily timed Army promotion of Captain Danford to the rank of Major. The concluding award of Yale's highest honors to André Tardieu, French High Commissioner to the United States, brought to its dramatic climax a scene of surpassing emotion, augmented as Professor Jepson, at the organ, broke spontaneously into the uplifting strains of the *Marseillaise*. Tardieu's eloquent response, recalling the historic friendship of the American and French Republics, was reserved for the Alumni Luncheon, where it was fittingly linked with the response of the British war-time Chaplain John Kelman, on whom Yale had just conferred the degree of Doctor of Divinity, recognizing in him "a voice from the trenches, interpreting the spiritual significance of war." In fullest harmony with the occasion and with Yale tradition were the opening address of President Hadley and the closing speech of former President William Howard Taft, at that time Kent Professor of Law at Yale. Thus ended a

Yale Commencement forever memorable in her annals, and a year fulfilled in the spirit of service, given final emphasis by President Taft in his concluding words—"For God, for Country, and for Yale."

Conclusion

The Yale Commencement on June 20, 1917, marked for the Torch Honor Society precisely six months since the first announcement of the Founding of Torch on December 20, 1916. Within the compass of that eventful half-year the new Honor Society had faced, in quick succession, the searching tests alike of peace and war. Conceived in terms of service to the normal interests of the campus, it had promptly met, and repeatedly anticipated, the imminent demands of war. In its response to the precedents of peace and to the unprecedented challenge of the First World War, the Torch Honor Society had doubly confirmed its birthright and widened the field of its purposeful activities.

Despite the early departures from college of most Torch undergraduates to enter elsewhere different fields of war training, eight of the twelve Torch Seniors received, either in person or *in absentia,* the regular Sheff degree of Bachelor of Philosophy upon the Graduation Day of the Class of 1917 S. They had satisfied the general and special requirements, whether scholastic or military, of their several courses of study, met in part by such anticipatory or special tests as had been individually required, and mainly by evidence of "good and regular standing" prior to departure for active service. The Ph.B. degree was at that period the comprehensive degree for three-year Sheff candidates, including those in the various Engineering groups and in the Select Course, then the largest of the Sheff groups.

On the Commencement programs of June 20, 1917, the list of recipients of the Ph.B. degree was headed by those awarded the degree "with distinction." In the group of three receiving the *Summa Cum Laude* distinction was John William Roy Crawford, Jr., who long before his departure for the Plattsburg R.O.T.C.

had been voted by his classmates their "most scholarly" member. On the regular Ph.B. list were seven other Torch Seniors: Samuel W. Atkins, Graham M. Brush, Farley Hopkins, H. Wiley Krotzer, Cord Meyer, Charles M. Sheldon, Jr., and Edward J. Winters. A month before Eddie Winters had won his lieutenancy in the Marine Corps. All the rest had left college early and were on their way to officers' commissions in their chosen forms of militant service. In the Commencement group were seven of the "First Ten" of the 1917 S. Torch delegation and one of the two members added as Seniors. Here again was illustrated that mating of the issues of peace and war incessantly emphasized in Torch experience.

In the unfolding history of the Torch Honor Society, the Yale Commencement of June 20, 1917 remains at once a terminal and a pivotal date. It closed a year marked by the formal advent of the new Sheff society and a half-year that exposed it constantly to tests crucial and unprecedented in Yale undergraduate life. In the confronting challenges of peace and war the character and contribution of the Torch enterprise stood manifest not alone on the Sheff campus and on the Yale scene but on the testing-grounds of national war-service. Facing forward now to the indefinite and uncertain future, the Torch knew that the past, at least, was secure. The attested faith, vision, and courage of the founders and followers of Torch gave heartening hope that, in the record of the Founding of the Torch Honor Society, history had also its prophetic function.

CPSIA information can be obtained at www.ICGtesting.com
Printed in the USA
BVOW03s1656150913

331206BV00007B/192/P